The Confessions Of The Countess Of Strathmore

Mary Eleanor Bowes Strathmore

THE

CONFESSIONS

OF THE

Countefs of Strathmore;

Mary Eleanor Lyon]

WRITTEN BY HERSELF.

CAREFULLY COPIED FROM

THE ORIGINAL,

LODGED IN

DOCTOR's COMMONS.

When hoary Age the luftful Paffions bend,
Compunction oft the Matron's bofom rend:
Then comes CONFESSION, eager to difclofe
The *fource* and *caufe* of all her prefent woes.

LONDON:

PRINTED FOR W. LOCKE, NO. 12, RED LION-STREET, HOLBORN.

1793.

CONFESSIONS.

I HAVE been guilty of five crimes.

The firſt, my unnatural diſlike to my eldeſt ſon, for faults which, at moſt, he could only be the innocent cauſe and not the author of: of this I have repented many months ago, and am moſt ſincerely ſorry I did not ſooner, in compliance with ſincere and moſt diſintereſted advice.

My ſecond crime was, my connection with Mr. Gray before Lord Strathmore's

B death;

death; in punifhment of which very crime, God blinded my judgment, that I could not difcern, in any cafe, what was for my children's and my own advantage; but in every thing where there were two expedients, I chofe the worft.

By medicines, I have reafon to think, I mifcarried three times, and attempted it the fourth; but, thank God, failed perpetrating that crime.

Next, I repent having profaned Saint Paul's and Weftminfter Abbey, by giving Mr. Gray meetings there, before Lord Strathmore's death; and that afterwards, inftead of ufing the influence I had over him to make him a better chriftian, I rather made him worfe.

Ano-

Another crime was, plighting myſelf moſt ſolemnly to Mr. Gray, at St. Paul's, to marry none but him; and yet I married you, which, together with my previous connection with you, I reckon amongſt my crimes,

I am now going to enumerate my imprudencies; firſt declaring, I have told you every crime I ever was guilty of, and that I never had a criminal connection with any perſon but yourſelf and Mr. Gray, and that Mr. James Graham was the only one, beſides, who could have ſtood the leaſt chance of ſucceeding in ſuch an attempt: yet violent as my paſſion was for him, I do ſtill ſincerely think it was pure; for my anxiety about his health and welfare continued two years after he left England, though I never ſaw or heard from him

during

during that time, or received a meſſage from him by his ſiſter above twice, though ſhe always wrote about him.

Of my imprudencies I ſhall now give you an exact account, under general heads, as you deſired; referring for your inſpection, in caſe you chuſe to ſee it, a moſt circumſtantial account of every thought and action of my life, which I am drawing up.

I was imprudent, though moſt innocent, both in thought and deed, in my flirtation—when quite a girl, with the Duke of Buccleugh's brother, which laſted but a very ſhort time. I was imprudent in marrying Lord Strathmore, againſt my mother's advice, though with her conſent.

I was

I was fo imprudent, as to give very improper encouragement to Mr. James Graham, and to give him reafon, by indirect, though plain words, to think that I had more than an affectionate friendfhip for him; and that I had once, I confefs, and was weak enough, during a fortnight that he lived under the fame roof, and were much together, to admit from him many improper declarations, not only without anger, but even with fatisfaction. After he went out of Scotland, I received one letter from him only, which I burnt to afhes, and drank them up for fear of any accident: I never wrote to him but once, which was in a feigned hand, and what none but himfelf could underftand: this was in a cover of his fifter's letter, which reached him all torn to pieces, and long after the time it ought; fo that it

was

was quite unintelligible, and never after that wrote to him except once, all before he left London. We often sent such meffages, as we could with safety, to each other, through his fifter's means; who all the time protefted fhe would not do fuch a thing, and made Mrs. Parifh believe the affection was all on my fide— that fhe wifhed to diffuade me from fuch thoughts, and refufed to write any meffage, which I believe fhe thinks to this moment; and that Mifs Graham is a moft virtuous woman and true friend, which is fo much, I know, the very reverfe of her character, that after I was thoroughly acquainted with it, nothing fhould have induced me to keep up a correfpondence, or the leaft acquaintance with her, but my paffion for her brother, and the ufe fhe was of to me in it.

At

At length I thought he ufed me very ill, and after complaining of it without redrefs (though I have reafon to believe Mifs G. concealed a letter, if not more, of his from me) I wrote a very violent letter to Mifs G. full of abufe of her bro-ther; and concluding, with defiring fhe would retail it to him, and add, that he might ' aller fe faire pendre.' This hurt her exceedingly, and having no occafion for fuch a troublefome woman, I was glad to get rid of her correfpondence.

When he came to fee me in London after this, (which was after Lord Strath-more's death) and waited on me, I would not fee him, and he attempted to throw himfelf in my way to no purpofe. I was then engaged to Mr. Gray, and having, at the rifk of my life, conquered my head-

headftrong paffion, I was determined not
to expofe myfelf to another conflict, with
one whom I had fo much reafon to be
afraid of.

I was more than imprudent in encou-
raging and keeping company with people
of fuch execrable and infamous princi-
ples: though, indeed, I did not think
them fuch then; but that is no excufe for
me, as I ought not to have trufted or allowed any body to have frequented my
houfe, without a previous long acquaintance. It was ftill worfe, to let George fo
much into my fecrets. As to my madnefs,
in wifhing Mrs. Stephens to ftay with me
after I was married, I can only fay, that
it was a diabolical infatuation, and that
had I known her as I do now, I fhould
not only have intreated you to turn her out

of

of the houfe directly; and have confeffed, that fuch a wretch was not fit to live on the earth; and had I known Mr. Stephens, who I took for an honeft, blunt man, I fhould have thought only with horror of his ever being near my fons, or in my houfe.

Going to the Conjuror's in Dean-ftreet, was a great imprudence, as alfo was con-fulting one three years before, on Lud-gate-hill (I think it was) where I went with Mrs. Planta and Mrs. Parifh, and alfo twice to a woman in Crown-court, once alone, and once with Mrs. Stephens: be-fides this, I confulted fome Gypfies in a barn, three fummers ago, at Paul's Wal-den, and three near there of different fets.

C

I was

I was imprudent to carry my revenge (as I then thought it) on the Planta family, so far as to advise Mrs. Stephens to marry against her confent, and to fend her off to Scotland, which I ought not to have done, even if she had been a good woman.

I had at this time a footman, one William Stamp, who (that I might not fo often appear to have letters from Mifs Graham) I ufed to fend now and then to Newcaftle, under pretence of feeing his brother who lived there (when I knew of a letter coming, which I often did before-hand) and bid him bring the letters to myfelf firft—but this was all he knew of the matter.

It was not till after many months of conftant attention, and many marks of fincerity and friendfhip, that, juft as I was going to Paul's Walden for two months,

(L. S.

(L. S. at Briftol) Mr. Gray ventured to give me fome verfes, which expreffed in a delicate, though rather in too tender a manner for mere friendfhip, his regard for me, and his great concern for my leaving London. From many circumftances, I had conceived fo high an opinion of the goodnefs of his heart and difpofition, that I was unwilling to lofe his friendfhip; fo that though I made no anfwer, I expreffed no anger, but continued correfponding with him openly and fairly till we both returned to town: foon after that, Lord S. went to Mr. Palgrave's, where he made fome ftay. One day juft after, as Mrs. Parifh and me were fitting at dinner, the poft brought me a letter from Mr. Lyon, in which he refufed, very uncivilly, to fend me a fmall fum of money, I told him I had written for by Lord S.'s directions;

and

and another letter from Mifs Graham, in which I found fhe had received a letter from her brother, who, as he began to do for fome time before, never fo much as mentioned me, but fpoke with the higheft commendations of a lady at Minorca, where he was arrived. As I was full of refentment at Mr. Lyon, and determined never more to think of Mr. James Graham, a fervant, (I don't recollect who, for I had no fecrets then) brought me a letter from Mr. Gray, who by an Enigma, very ingenioufly invented, had pitched upon that very day to fee how far he might venture: if I was angry, he might have explained it away; but if I underftood it, or pretended not to underftand it, then he might fpeak plainer. I chofe the latter method, and, full of refentment, thought I had revenged myfelf

on

on others, whilft I was literally on myfelf:
as I felt nothing for Mr. G. that exceeded
friendfhip, or gave me caufe to apprehend
the confequences of fuch a connection,
I confented to accept the love of a man,
whom I could always keep within bounds,
and whom I had conceived fuch an efteem
for, that I reckoned his friendfhip a comfort
I fhould be very forry to lofe. I faw him
three times when I knew Mrs. Parifh was
at the Mufeum, and met him for a fhort
time, as if by accident, at the Ring, without, I really believe, any fufpicion; but
as Lord S. was out of town—was expect-
ed foon to return, he preffed me to fee
him oftener at my houfe, and meet him
oftener at different places abroad; but this
was found impracticable without trufting
fomebody; and unfortunately, after taking
what we thought all neceffary precautions,

we

we agreed to truft George, whofe fecrecy
and caution, we both thought we had reafon to be fatisfied with: we imprudently
allowed him to tell us freely all the reports
of the town, on every occafion, where
either were in the leaft concerned.

He once, I am convinced, from fome
interefted motive, rendered us a material
fervice in preventing, by a ready turn, it's
being detected that he was in the houfe.
In this manner we went on till Lord S. returned to town, and he went to Bath,
agreeing not to correfpond till I wrote to
tell him he might return, which I did in
a month's time, when Lord S. went away,
but did not fee him for fome days, I cannot recollect how many, but once in that
month he came up to town, and contrived
to convey me a note, letting me know, that

his

his impatience had made him disobey my
orders, and come up to town without a
summons, just to see me for an hour
or two. He therefore begged I would
meet him at Lever's, as by accident, which
I did, and he returned directly to Bath,
where he staid till I wrote to him to return. The weather being extremely se-
vere the day before he went to Bath, and
I having met him very early in Saint
James's Park, my shoes extremely wet,
and bottom of my petticoats, and I not
having leisure to change them for some
time after I came home, I caught a slow
fever, and cut myself dreadfully by fall-
ing on the ice; so that I was ill when I
went to Lever's, where I encreased my
complaints; and just after Lord S. went
away, I fell into an ague, in my face, from
which I suffered for near a month, half

of

of every twenty-fours hours such torments, as nothing but the disorder I had just after my marriage, can in any degree be compared to: my head swelled so, yet without easing my pain, that I was blind, and even spoke with pain. In this miserable condition, Mr. G. visited me every evening unknown, as I thought by all but George, who let him in, and unsuspected by all but Mrs. Parish, who sometimes remonstrated, but very gently, and I turned it off with a laugh or joke: at first, she thought it only flirtation, and then she said nothing; for there is not, with all her pretended gravity and prudence, so great a coquette, or one so easily flattered, even on her beauty, as she is; which, if you doubt, I can bring you many undeniable proofs. Witness for one thing, how

Alexan-

Alexander Nairne made her appear ridiculous.

I omitted to mention, in its proper place, that I told Mr. Gray he had my friendſhip and eſteem ; that my heart had long been in poſſeſſion of another, from whom I had determined to withdraw it, but had done it ſo ſhort a time, that I ſhould think it an injury againſt the friendſhip and confidence he was entitled to, if I concealed this circumſtance from him : alſo, that I had been ſo unhappy in matrimony, that I was determined never to engage myſelf indiſſolubly, though I would moſt faithfully, if, on theſe conditions, he would be ſatisfied with my affection, he ſhould have it entire if Lord S. died; that if he recovered, he muſt give me up; and that during my huſband's

life,

life; he muſt decline all thoughts of me.
To all this with reluctance, and finding
me peremptory, he conſented, and gave
me his promiſe, which he ſtrictly kept till
I was juſt recovered, when I found he ex-
pected to be rewarded, for the very great
attentions (by writing to me all day, and
ſitting by me all the evening) which he
conſtantly paid during my confinement:
and one unfortunate evening I was off my
guard, and ever after that (the middle of
February) I lived occaſionally with him as
his wife; and from that time, till my
connection with you, I declare, I never
had a thought of any other man.

I was once with child by him, before I
heard of Lord S.'s death, which I did not
till the 6th of April; but was ſo frighten-
ed and unhappy at it, that I prevailed on
him

him to bring me a quack medicine he had
heard of for mifcarriage, but never tried
it: it was of a coperas fubftance, by the
tafte and look; he gave it me very re-
luctantly, as he faid he did not know but
it might be poifon; however, I would
have it.

All the time of my connection with
Mr. Gray, precautions were taken; but
an inftant's neglect always deftroyed them
all: indeed, fometimes, even when I
thought an accident fcarcely poffible.

My folly was unpardonable, in trufting Mr. and Mrs. Stephens, George Stephens, Mr. Matra, Mr. Magra, Mr. Pemberton, (whom I once actually told I was
married to Mr. Gray) and, above all things,
George, in talking of my affairs and in-

tentions

-tentions fo freely before them. I alfo depended moft fatally on Mr. Peele's honefty; and, three or four times, added a few lines in too free and jocofe a ftile to Mr. Stephens, in the letters Mrs. Stephens wrote him: he anfwered thefe paragraphs in her letter, which fhe fhewed me. To the beft of my recollection, I never wrote to Mr. Stephens, but in his wife's letters, which I read to her, or fhewed her, and was added on the fame paper fhe wrote on; and he never wrote to me any other way; (all this was only whilft he was at Winchefter, except once that he wrote only to myfelf) having wrote to her the poft before, which was a fulfome letter about his wife, who, I told him, had not been well, (which was true) owing, I believe, to his abfence: and, I proteft, I thought fo then.

This

This letter was chiefly, if not folely, expreffing his anxiety for her health, and dependance on my friendly care: I burnt this, with feveral other letters, a few days after I received it. This moment I recollect I have made a miftake; for I had a letter of thanks from him whilft he was on the expedition to Scotland. I had once a letter from Mr. G. Stephens, excufing himfelf from dining with me that day, according to invitation, as he was obliged to leave town on particular bufinefs. I correfponded conftantly with Mr. Pemberton for fome years; and as he writes well, I have moft, if not all, his letters in London, (and the few I had from Captain Magra) at leaft, I had when I came down here laft; for I faw them amongft my papers when I came down to the election. All Dr. Brown's letters, feveral letters of

bufinefs

bufinefs to, and copies of letters from me, and fome others lefs material, were all removed before my return, and without my order. I wifh I had fome of Dr. Brown's letters; for they might have done me credit if feen.

When Mr. Stephens was at Winchefter, I advifed Mrs. Stephens to take a vomit, thinking fhe was with child; as I had taken a ridiculous notion into my head, that having children made a man like his wife lefs.

According to Mifs Graham's defire and to prevent accidents, I burnt all the letters I had from her as faft as they came; which I have fince repented of. I alfo burnt all Mr. Gray's letters from the fame fear: I mean only thofe which I received before

Lord

Lord Strathmore's return from Mr. Palgrave's.

I was always extremely filly, in not minding reports; on the contrary, rather encouraged them; partly, that I might laugh at other people's abfurdities and credulity, and partly, becaufe I left it to time and reafon, to fhew they were falfe, and thought a variety of reports would puzzle people; fo that they would look upon every one relating to me, as equally falfe, and even not credit the truth. Whereas, I have fince had reafon to fear it had quite a contrary effect from what I imagined and intended.

I foolifhly let George tell me all the ridiculous ftories he heard about Mr. Gray and myfelf, and other people, fo far as

they

they related to us: and we ufed to laugh at them; and as he was to have been our courier, when we went abroad, which was fixed for the 8th or 10th of April, to ftay two, three, or more years; I ufed to let him afk me any French words he did not underftand, as he knew that language. I gave him, the day or two before my marriage, the deed drawn up on account of my intended marriage with Mr. Gray, along with a vaft heap of papers and let-ters, and an old leafe or two of the houfe, of little or no confequence, and bid him put them all into the kitchen fire; but before he could get there, called him back, and after fwearing him to fecrefy, bid him only burn the papers, and keep the deed till I called for, or bid him burn it.

I declare

I declare solemnly, I did not do this from any miftruft in your generofity or honour. How could I? For I had a high opinion of both, and had never feen or heard (except your behaviour to Mrs. Stoney, which I believed to be only county of Durham malice) any thing which induced me to think otherwife: befides, as I yielded all my fortune without any referve for myfelf, and as I am very far from an extravagant woman, I never had a doubt, you would chearfully fupply me with what fums I might want, which would be very fmall indeed after my debts were paid, which I have often wifhed I could have done before I married. Therefore, you fee my doubt could by no means concern myfelf: but it ftruck me, that having taken fuch precautions on my children's

E   account,

account, (for whom I was anſwerable, though not for myſelf) with a man who I knew I could truſt; I ought not to be leſs cautious with one whom I could not be ſo ſtrongly aſſured of: but I would not tell you of the paper, leſt it ſhould look like miſtruſt.

Your fondneſs for my children, and the generoſity I thought I diſcovered in you, on all occaſions relating to pecuniary matters; together with the apparent openneſs of your temper, which was very bearable till long after that, made me aſſure myſelf I had nothing to fear for my children, and reproach my heart, for ever having entertained a ſhadow of a doubt. Therefore, before we came to the election, I ordered George to burn the paper; and

and when we were at Gibſide, I once
aſked him if he had; and he declared he
had: but not content with that, I had
written three or four lines in French when
I told him, (not having time to tell him
when I ſpoke to him) that I charged him
never to reveal having had that deed, or of
any other thing he knew relating to me;
and threatened him if he did. This was
madneſs, and thank God I changed my
mind and burnt the paper, (for whilſt I
heſitated, I believe he went away) elſe he
might have ſhewn that paper to Mr. Lyon:
ſo chance ſtood my friend, I confeſs, and
not prudence.

I told you, if I don't greatly miſtake or
forget, that I gave Mr. Stephens 1000l.
within a month or ſix weeks before my marriage with you, but that I could not ſpeak

certainly

certainly as to the time. I have since re-
collected that I told you wrong. About
that time, I gave Mrs. Stephens a sum for
her own use, of 50l. or 100l. (I cannot be
positive which, but I think the latter) and
this must have been what misled me.——
Something you said since you came to
Gibside——I think it was his being so com-
municative, and speaking his opinion so
blunt to every body——reminded me of the
mistake I had made: would I had told
you of it then; but I foolishly, out of
fear of your anger, delayed telling you
till now: It was the very evening of the
day I was married, that I gave Mrs. Stephens, and not Mr. Stephens, the 1000l.
which I desired she would accept for herself and him, in performance of a pro-
mise I had made him the day (the first I
ever saw him) before he went off with
that

that more than woman, that I would pay
his debts; he having told me at that time,
which I remember greatly prejudiced me
in his favour, that he had debts to the
amount of fome hundred pounds, and
that he could not be eafy in his mind, if
he entered into an engagement with Mrs.
Stephens; and therefore lived in my family (as I told him he was to do) without
letting us know how he was fituated.
This, together with the affection he took
that opportunity of expreffing for his laft
wife, made me rejoice in having met with
fuch a perfon. I told him, if he made
Mrs. Stephens a good hufband, and behaved
in the manner I had no doubt he would,
I would take care he fhould have no trouble from his debts—I really believe he
made her a good hufband, (I ftill believe
he does a better than fhe deferves, I am
fure

fure he cannot a worfe) and I gave her,
the evening of the day I married you,
1000l. to give him, doubting not that
would be a pleafing ftep to both, and en-
dear her more to him. His apparent fincerity and honeft freedom in expoftulat-
ing with me, when I told him I was married to you, pleafed and affected me greatly, and moved me to a fincere forrow and
penitence. I thought it became a Cler-
gyman and an honeft one, and I thought
him fincere and honeft in what he faid,
and that he rifked his fortune to fpeak
truth: even when him and his wife went
to France, I actually thought them — to that
very time, but no longer, from fome hints
you directly after that let drop—fincere
and faithful friends to both you and me,
and grieved you did not treat them better;
fuch was my infatuation. May Mr. S.
forgive

forgive me, the fad wretch I unknowingly
gave him.

It was the night, or two nights after
this; the night Mrs. S. and Mrs. C. S.
came from Paul's Walden, that I fat up
with Mr. George Stephens till two o'clock
(I think it was) in the morning, which
gave you fuch offence. Our whole converfation was about you; he was of a
different opinion from his brother, who
he faid thought and fpoke like a Parfon,
but not like a gentleman of unprejudiced
education; a man of nice honour and
delicate feelings. He commended what
I had done, which he faid he never fhould
have doubted my doing, had he not believed I was previoufly married. He
commended me much, and blamed Mr.
Gray. This, and obfervations and accounts

counts of what happened at Paul's Walden, was the whole purport of our converfation that night, which was the only particular, or fo circumftantial one, I ever had with him in my life.

As to Mr. Stephens, I believe it is needlefs to tell you, I never faw him before Mr. Matra introduced him to me; and Mr. Matra was introduced by the commendation of his brother, the Captain, and by the very ftrong ones of Dr. Solander.

As to Mrs. Parifh, fhe provoked me by an uninterrupted feries of ill-temper, deceit, felf-intereftednefs, and ingratitude; with obftinacy, and in many refpects a bad method with my children; and I found fhe mifled and mis-informed me

in

in the objects of my charity; in short,
she was too infufferable, elfe I would have
retained her. But, as I owe her nothing,
and she much to me, I shall say no more
about her.

I cannot be positive as to the month,
but think it muft have been in October,
when I went to the Conjuror in Pear-
ftreet. Mrs. Stephens, Mr. Pennick, Mr.
Matra (all of whom I think breaftfafted
with me that morning) were of the party,
and Capt. Magra met us, I thing half way.
Mrs. Stephens told me of a Conjuror at
the Old Bailey, who she had been to; and
I had a curiofity to fee him. Accordingly,
we walked to the Old Bailey, where we
met a little boy, who came up to us and
afked if we wanted the gentleman who fo
many people came after, and that he

F   would

would conduct us to him? we said yes, and he carried us through blind alleys to Pear-ftreet: Mrs. Stephens told me afterwards it was not the man fhe had been to before. It was between 11 and 12, as near as I can recollect, when we got to Pear-ftreet, and there were fuch a number of people in the room we waited in, to whom the Conjuror was firft engaged, and they took fo long a time to have their fortunes told, that it was almoft 6 o'clock before they began with us; and Capt. Magra and felf were weak enough to go down twice to the cellar or room below ftairs, where he fat. Capt. Magra, who went down in perfect unbelief, came up convinced of the man's knowledge from what he told him. The two brothers, Mrs. Stephens, Mr. Pennick, and myfelf, returned in a hackney-coach, which

which was called in Smithfield, from
Pear-ftreet to Grofvenor-fquare, or very
near it, I forgot which; and I did not get
home till paft eight o'clock, almoft ftarved
to death with cold and hunger; for it
was with great difficulty we procured, a
little before we came away, a little bad
bread and water, and two logs of green
wood, which we put in a chimney-place
where there was no grate, and which
gave very little warmth, in a cold rainy
day, to the coldeft room I ever was in,
and which had no other furniture than
two (or three at moft) rotten chairs, and a
wooden trunk. I went by the name of
the widow Smith, and Mrs. Stephens, and
Mr. Pennick, by fome other, which I
cannot at prefent recollect, though I have
endeavoured to do it. During the firft
part of the time we were waiting, Mr.

Pennick

Pennick wrote fome verfes (and repeated feveral quotations) which begun with,

" Thro' Dirty-ftreet we bent our way,
" To have our Fortunes told to-day (or this day.")

To the beft of my recollection, there were eight or ten more of the fame fort of lines followed thefe, but of which I could not for my life recollect one word, any more than of two or four (I believe four) lines I wrote likewife on the partition, which contained fome reflection on a general head; to the beft of my remembrance, it was againft matrimony; I am fure, at leaft I think I am, that I fhould recollect them if I faw them again, and I would tell you. Before we went away, we rubbed all the verfes out with our fingers fo carefully, that I can fwear that none but the two which you fhewed me

were

were poffibly legible, and they not without the greateft difficulty, the pencil being
blacker as they were firft written, I fup-
pofe was the reafon they were plainer.
Mr. Magra, and I think Mr. Pennick, ftaid
fupper; and I believe it was nearer one
than twelve when they went away : I cannot recollect whether Mr. Gray fupped
with me that night, but I know he did
not dine in Grofvenor-fquare. Mrs. Stephens fung and played from dinner till
fupper, and afterwards we laughed at the
adventures of the day. When we were
at the Conjuror's waiting, a variety of
ftrange citizens, &c. came in and out, as
there was but one anti-chamber for us
all: the gentlemen entered into converfa-
tion with them all, but I only fpoke to
two ; the firft a woman, the beft and moft
decent looking, who told me her hiftory,

and

and her repenting of not taking the Conjuror's advice, who she confulted two or
three times, or oftener, in a year. I paffed myfelf upon her for a Grocer's widow,
and was come to confult the Conjuror,
whether I fhould marry a Brewer, or Su-
gar-boiler, who propofed to me amongft
others, and I had ten children. Mrs.
Stephens alfo fpoke, the only one I think
fhe did. The other perfon I fpoke to,
was a little Portuguefe Jew, about 15
years old, whofe father, a rich broker, or
pawnbroker, Capt. Magra knew; and we
two fpoke to him in Spanifh, though not
much: his father had fent him to find
out who ftole fome of his filver fpoons.
It is impoffible a more exact or true account of this filly affair can be given, than
is now before you.

In

In the courſe of this long ſtory, three or four trifling circumſtances eſcaped my memory, ſo that I cannot place them under the proper heads they belonged to, and now they will appear totally unconnected; but as I profeſs (and moſt ſincerely) to omit not one circumſtance, either material or trifling, and that is the only merit I pretend or wiſh for in this Narration ; I ſhall attend to exactneſs, and not regularity, which you will perceive I have all along too much neglected, having written things exactly as they preſented themſelves to my memory.

When Mr. Scot gave me the blue ring, I gave him one my father had given me, exactly the ſame, by which means nobody perceived I had got a new ring, and this none knew but ourſelves. I endeavoured

to

to perfuade Mr. Liddle, by hints, &c. it was the Duke of Buccleugh and not his brother, whom I had a liking for, and puzzled him, that he fometimes thought the Duke, and fometimes Mr. Scot.

When I went to the Park, Kenfington Gardens, or any way in the ftreet to meet Mr. Gray, I forgot to mention that George walked behind me, and therefore knew of it; alfo when I went to the Gypfies and Conjuror's.

When I mentioned William Stamp, I likewife forgot to tell you that twice or thrice, in paying him a bill, I gave him fome money (a guinea or two at moft) over what was due, under pretence of rewarding his diligence as a fervant, but, in fact, as a bribe (though I did

not

not tell him fo) not to fpeak of the letters he brought, as I told you, from New-caftle.

N. B. It had almoft flipt my memory to tell you that Lord S.'s beauty, which was then very great, and a dream or rather vifion, to which I was foolifh enough to give more credit than it deferved, were two great inducements to me to marry Lord S.

One thing more, and I have quite done. I do affure you, you did me great injuftice in thinking thofe fits were affected to which I have fo many years been fubject, and from which I have fuffered fo much at various times. The laft I had, alfo the night before Dr. Scott left Gibfide, was indeed real; but I confefs, that out

G   of

of fulkinefs for what you had faid to me that day, I did not fpeak or anfwer you fo foon as I was able.

I have now punctually, minutely, and moft entirely given you a full account of every thing I ever did, faid, or thought, that was wrong.

I have, under my own hand, furnifhed you with a perpetual fund for unkindnefs, and even good excufe for bad ufage; but you are my hufband—I obey you, and if you continue to diftruft, abufe, and think of me as you have hitherto done, Providence muft and will decide which of us two is moft to blame.

I know, according to your promife, you will never again repeat paft griev-
ances;

ances; but if you think of them I shall
suffer as much and more from the unkindnefs, your brooding filently over them will
conftantly create; for indeed I fear you
are of an unforgiving, and in this respect
unforgetting temper; else you could not,
for fo many months together, have behaved fo uniformly cruel to one whofe
whole wifh and ftudy was to pleafe you.

If you think my fincerity and unre-
ferved confeffion of my faults may entitle
me to afk a favour, let me beg your promife to burn thefe papers, at leaft that you
will deftroy them when I die, that I may
not ftand condemned and difgraced, under
my own hand, to pofterity.

I am going to fulfil my promife of lay-
ing before you all the crimes and foibles
of my life. To prove that I am fincere,

G 2 I know

I know not what method to take. I cannot make any imprecations on myfelf, as
I am already fo loaded with mifery, that
there is only one curfe which is not mine
already. Therefore, I only wifh that one
may happen to me, if I do not fpeak (without the leaft extenuation) the whole and
exact truth : that I do this I can only refer
to a long feries of fufferings and patience to
prove, if it pleafe God to give me ftrength
and refolution to trail out my exiftence till
even you are convinced, by my example,
that a perfon who has once been vicious,
may repent and become good.

I am convinced that the want of a proper fenfe of religion has been the original
caufe of all my errors ; all the grounds
of this mifchief was laid before my father
died, and then I was only between eleven
and

and twelve years old. My father was the youngeft of four fons, and intended for a profeffion, but never would give his mind in the leaft to ftudy; on the contrary, when only eighteen he ran away, and laid out what money his mother had given him for other purpofes, in buying a com- miffion in the army, where he continued 'till he came to the eftate. As he was uncommonly handfome, and a great rake in his youth, he grew very pious in his advanced years, and having felt the want of education and ftudy, for he was (as I have heard him fay) determined his heir fhould not feel the fame inconveniences; accord- ingly, he brought me up with a view to my being as accomplifhed at thirteen, as his favourite firft wife was at that age, in every kind of learning, except Latin.

At

At four years old I could read uncommonly well, and was kept tight to it, made to get many things off by heart. I read the Bible, but at the same time equal or greater pains were taken to inftruct me in the Mythology of every Heathen nation that ever exifted; and my father, who was a real patriot and a brave man, was continually expatiating on the patriotic virtues, and fhining merits of the ancient philofophers and heroes. My mind was fo puzzled with fuch a variety of religions, that, except the firm belief of a God, I knew not which of all the modes of worfhip to adopt from real conviction; as to the weak judgment of a child, all appeared equally fupported by tradition. However, I faw my father was a chriftian, and a proteftant, therefore I called and believed myfelf one too, though it is not

till

till within thefe few months that I have had leifure, compofure, and inclination to inveftigate thefe matters; and now I am become a chriftian from conviction,

Another misfortune for me, was, that though my father did not applaud fuicide and revenge in general terms, by their names; I have often heard him fpeak highly of men who have been guilty of them; Cato for one inftance. My father's whole care and attention was beftowed on the improvement of my knowledge, in whatever I fhewed a genius for; and in acquiring me a great ftock of health, hardening and ftrengthening my confti-tution by every poffible means, often the moft rigid ones. My father was continu-ally talking of, and endeavouring to incul-cate into me, fentiments of generofity,

grati-

gratitude, fortitude, and duty to himſelf, and an inſatiable thirſt for all kinds of knowledge. But I never heard him once ſay, to the beſt of my recollection, that chaſtity, patience, and forgiveneſs of injuries, were virtues; and he was very paſſionate. During his life, my mother did not interfere with my education. When I was between eleven or twelve years old, he died. Amongſt other things, my father made me ſpeak ſpeeches before much company, and get moſt part of Ovid's Metamorphoſes by heart, as well as Milton, &c. My mother ſtaid at Gib-ſide, where my father died, till I was near thirteen. We went then to London and ſtaid till I was fourteen, ſhe continuing all that time in ſuch affliction, as to be incapable of attending either to my education or mo-rals: for the former ſhe relied on the beſt maſter,

mafter, and my own defire of learning, and
for my conduct, fhe relied on an old maid-
en aunt, Mrs. J. B. who came up to town,
and till I married I lived chiefly with her.
This woman firft introduced me into the
world, when my mother could not go out.
She had been a celebrated beauty, and extremely vain; but, unfortunately for me,
of nothing more, than having a niece who
was one of the greateft fortunes in England; and (though I ought not to fay it,
nor do I but with confufion and fhame,
that I did not employ my talents better)
a prodigy of learning. Mrs. Montague,
amongft others, was pleafed to honour me
with her friendfhip, approbation, and correfpondence, (I can yet fhew feveral of
her letters) and this continued without in-
terruption till Lord S. after my marriage,
obliged me to break off with her, in a

H   very

very rude and abrupt manner, (going no more to her Sundays, and only once a year rapping at her door) telling me fhe was a wild, light, filly woman, of bad character, and not fit for my acquaintance. Sadly againft my inclination, I was forced to comply, and give her up, with many others.

But, to return to my aunt: fhe was for two years (after which I returned under my mother's care) fo indulgent a chaperon, that I muft fay, if I had not been more prudent than moft young girls of my age, I might have been lefs fo.

The firft imprudence I ever was guilty of, was carrying on for twelve months a flirtation with Mr. Scott, the Duke of Buccleugh's brother, whom I frequently met

and

and danced with at children's balls, as
they were called, and chiefly at the Du-
chefs of Northumberland's. Girls and
boys were admitted from five or fix, to
fourteen or fifteen years old. I was thirteen when this began, and Mr. Scott was
a year or two older, I cannot be fure
which. He liked my converfation, and
as he was fmart and clever, I liked his;
and all this would have only been a flirtation, I really believe, had not my filly
coufin, Liddell, who was his fchool-fellow,
and was ftaying with my mother, teazed
us into a belief that we were in love with
each other; however, no further engagement paffed between us than that he told
me he had a tender affection for me, and
liked my company better than any other
girl's; at which I was not difpleafed,
but in return, I particularly remember I made ufe of the words, " ten-

der efteem for him." He went foon after into the army, and before he fet out for Germany afked me to exchange rings with him, which I readily agreed to; and you know and have often feen the ring. He died about a twelve month after he went abroad, of the fmall pox, in the natural way.

N. B. The prefent Mr. Charles Fox had a great liking for me, and followed me, but had too much pride to tell me fo directly, as he faw I preferred Mr. Scott, for which reafon, I know, he abufed both.

This affair of Scott's, was a great imprudence, but, thank God, no worfe.

After I recovered the fhock of Mr. Scott's death, whofe mother, Lady Dalkeith, hurt me much by her unfeelingnefs; I amufed myfelf, till I engaged to

marry

marry Lord S. with alternate ftudy and di-
verfions; fuch as public places, &c. I
had, I do affure you, no partiality for any
man in the world, though I had a great
many offers made to my mother for me;
as I told every body who offered, that I
fhould not hear any thing on that fubject
from any perfon, as all offers of that
kind muft come through my mother: accordingly, they all found themfelves obliged to apply to her; by which conduct,
I was both efteemed an uncommon prudent girl, and had the fatisfaction of refufing a great many people of rank, in
fuch due form as flattered my vanity, and
made it impoffible they could deny (as
they might otherwife) that they had offered to me. And fo great was my repu-
tation for prudence in thefe refpects, that
though a young Venetian Marquis, with

my

my mother's acknowledged confent and approbation, attended on me for near a twelve month, to all public places as Cicefbeo, and was frequent in his vifits at our houfe, the world did us juftice in believing this connection was entirely owing to my mother; and wifhing me to be perfect in the Italian language, and to his fpeaking Englifh fo very badly, that he could keep no company, but fuch as fpoke Italian (for his French was little better) and the number of thofe was ftill much more inconfiderable at that period than it is now, efpecially amongft the ladies. My mother was always partial to the Italian nation and their language. The Marquis, who was on his travels through Europe, proceeded to Paris, and fo we parted with the fame civility and indifference as we met: he fent my two little dogs from Paris;

wrote

wrote once or twice from France, and
once from Peterſburgh; ſince when, I have
heard nothing of or from him.

I gave ſome encouragement to Lord
Strathmore, but it was ſlight, though more
than to others: he wrote a letter to me
with a declaration; and having, as I afterwards found, tried unſuccefsfully, many
ways to get it conveyed to me, ſent it by
Mrs. Baker, who came under a pretence
of ſpending a day or two with my mother, who, at that time, hated the ſight of
her, and never aſked her to ſtay all night,
as ſhe thought her very officious, in ſpeak-
ing much, and greatly, in praiſe of the
Lord Strathmore's family; as my mother
thought, (though ſhe never poſitively told
me ſo) I ſhewed more partiality to Lord S.
than to any other perſon. Mrs. Baker took

an

an opportunity, when fhe was out of the
room, to give me Lord S 's letter; I guefl-
ed what it was, but, after reading a few
of the firft lines, returned it to Mrs. B.
telling her, I would not receive any letters
in that manner, and I thought the office
fhe had undertaken very unbecoming of
her, or any gentlewoman; and that the
gentleman, whofe name I had not looked
at, or was defirous to know, (here fhe in-
terrupted me and faid it was Lord S.) muft
apply to my mother, if he meant to have
any anfwer. I then left her under great
mortification; but I did not tell my mother
what had paffed, from an apprehenfion,
that it might fet her more againft my marrying Lord S ; and, becaufe fhe was fo
referved, that fhe did not treat even me,
with the confidence, I think, a daughter
entitled to. Therefore, I never durft open
my

my heart to, or confult upon thefe fub-
jects; and to this I attribute, in a great
meafure, the chief of my misfortunes
through life. Indeed, I muft fay, I was
always a dutiful child to her, till I was
married, and I have often heard her
own it.

Soon after Lord S. received my anfwer
from Mrs. Baker, he came to Gibfide, and
made his propofals in form to my mother,
who told him, fhe would acquaint me,
and as we were going directly to London,
for which place he alfo was going to fet
out, he fhould have his anfwer there: but
fhe did not tell me of his having offered,
till two days after he had left the houfe;
and then affected to mention it as a thing
fhe did not doubt I fhould refufe; as, fhe
faid, there were three objections; diforder

I   in

in the family; a mother, and many brothers and fifters, whom, perhaps, I fhould find troublefome ; and, laftly, (the chief with her) his being a Scotchman. The firft, I had often heard, was only a falfe report, and believed fincerely it proceeded from envy, ill nature, and partly fpite: the fecond, would afford me an opportunity of endearing myfelf to my hufband, whofe relations, I never doubted, would behave well to me; and the third, was a recommendation, as I had always a much greater partiality for the Scotch and Irifh, than for the Englifh.

I accordingly told her, that I had no objection to Lord Strathmore; but, that if her's were infuperable, I would not marry without her confent—only claimed the privilege of not marrying at all;

which,

which, in that cafe, I was determined
on. She then gave her confent, and faid,
fhe would tell Lord S. when he came to
town, as agreed on; and he went to town
directly. I muft not omit here to mention, that Mrs. Parifh, then my governefs,
fpoke greatly againft Lord S.

His favourite uncle, Charles Lyon,
taking a fever, and dying juft after we left
the country, detained Lord S. fo long from
coming up to London to receive this,
and as he durft not write, I did not
know the caufe, that I thought myfelf
flighted. Though grieved and provoked,
I put on a cheerful countenance, and
danced frequently at Almack's, with various people who followed me; though
they had not then declared themfelves:
amongft thefe, the moft affiduous were

Lord

Lord Mountſtuart and Mr. Chaloner. I
gave neither of them encouragement; yet
they contrived one night to quarrel, and
put the whole room in an uproar at Almack's, about who ſhould ſit next me at
ſupper. Both went out in a paſſion; a
challenge was given, but prevented by one
of the gentlemen (I believe Mr. Chaloner,
but never could be ſure which) aſking par-
don. Lady Mountſtuart, then Miſs Wind-
for, ſat one ſide of me, and having even
then a partiality for Lord M.S. begged me to
take notice of and encourage him, as he
was like a madman, and expoſed himſelf
to all the company, I confeſs, I did, with
a premeditated deſign, ſhew great civility
to Lady Bute and her daughters, one night
at Almack's, in order, that before Lord S.
arrived, and my engagement to him was
known, I might have an opportunity of
refuſing

refufing Lord M. S. This civility, which Lady Bute conftrued into encouragement, had the defired effect; and over-reached her great caution and pride (which I knew fhe had) in not offering, with a chance of her fon's being refufed: next morning fhe waited on my mother, to propofe for her fon, and met a mortification which hurt her much; and made him keep his bed for a week. This I confefs, was down-right girlifhnefs, mifchievoufnefs, and vanity.

My marriage treaty with Lord S. for one delay or other, trailed on about a year and a half; during which, I found our tempers, difpofitions, and turns different I wifhed to retract (and would, if I durft have confulted with my mother) but my pride, and fometimes my weaknefs, would

not

not let me: at length we were married,
at Paul's Walden, and I was brought a
fortnight after to Gibfide; though I had
began to be ill, juft before I fet out, as
two or three of the party had fluxes at
Paul's Walden; which we attributed to
my mother's bad Port-wine. I faid, though
I never tafted but one glafs of it, that it
had alfo affected me, in a moft dangerous
and poifonous manner, by a partial erup-
tion; though I don't believe the doctors
were, or could be, impofed upon.

I intended candidly, and in the fulleft
manner, to lay before you every action of
my life, relative to the leaft imprudence I
ever was guilty of: I have written a good
deal; but as you are impatient, and per-
ceiving I labour under a load of imputa-
tions, yet unknown to me, though cre-
dited

dited by you, many of which, I dare fay,
are falfe; I fhall, till after this is finifhed,
leave the trifling things, which were only
inadvertencies any girl might be and is
guilty of; and haften to tell you, in as
few words as poffible, every imprudence,
and every crime, I have been guilty of,
fince my marriage with Lord Strathmore,
which is as far back as I imagine you are
immediately anxious to know.

I had by him all my five children; and
during that time, never had one thought,
did one action, or faid one word, which
Heaven might not know without blaming
me, or indeed himfelf; except the dif-
like I had but too much caufe to entertain for Mr. Lyon. Before I had been
many months married, however, I put up
with that, and the difagreeable behaviour

of

of the reft of the family, and concealed
it as much as poffible from the world, till
he publicly, and caufelefsly, as many can
witnefs, infulted me in the public rooms
at Edinburgh, where I was with him and
Mrs. Lyon, who was juft married, all
the race-week without Lord Strathmore;
during which time, he behaved in fuch a
manner, as fcandalized the whole town of
Edinburgh; who, at that time, hated him
as much as they liked and pitied me. I
complained mildly to Lord Strathmore
about his brother; but it was an unfortunate and moft prejudiced rule with him,
that Mr. Lyon could not err; fo I got no
other redrefs than his faying, that though
he was hafty, he had a good heart, and
never meant to offend. I never complained to my mother on any occafion of
Lord S. or his family; but, on the contrary,

trary, expreffed an uncommon regard for both, of which fhe was jealous, and made her believe they ufed me extremely well: for as I had married him againft her advice, my pride would not let me complain, had they ufed me ten times worfe.

The year before this, Mr. Robert Graham, of Fuitry, took all opportunities to be in my company, and to exprefs, though not improperly, his regard and attention to me. He once told me fo pofitively, and received fuch an anfwer as was proper, and which, from my foolifh flirting with him, I dare fay he did not expect. He went from Glames in a pet, and being a man of violent refentments (which in all inftances have turned out againft himfelf) he directly propofed to Mifs Peggy Mylne, who always had a penchant for him; but

K   whom

whom he had taken every opportunity,
both in public and private, to abufe in a
moft groundlefs and violent manner; and
to profefs, that he would rather die than
marry her: yet fhe confented—they were
married fuddenly without his parents confent.

The year before, when I was on a vifit
to his mother, I faw for the firft time, and
not again for two years, his youngeft
brother, James; he was quite a boy, but
a very extraordinary one, and I muft confefs, much too forward for his years, and
too confcious of thofe fhining talents,
which no heart can, in fome degree without difficulty, be proof againft, when he
chofe to exert his art. I have the greateft
reafon to think, he, from that time, form-
ed a defign of enjoying my affections: he
made

made many attempts to come with his
other brothers to Glamis; but they con-
stantly, as Mifs Graham told me, refufed
to bring him: and he introduced himfelf,
or rather in a manner forced himfelf in,
to come to Glamis one day with his fifter;
when fhe walked to Bridge Town, fcarce
three miles from Glamis, where fhe, and
indeed myfelf, often ufed to go, to fee an
amiable and elegant woman, one Mrs.
Douglas, wife to my dear Emilia's brother; where he fometimes, and particularly at that time, was ftaying.   He, as I
afterwards found, offered to fet her home
to Glamis, when fhe was ftaying with me,
but fhe would not let him; upon which
he told her, there were droves of horned
cattle on the road, as it was the high road
to Forfar, where he told her it was mar-
ket-day; and knowing her extreme timi-

dity in that refpect, he was fure fhe would
not refufe him. She did not, and as he
has a confummate affurance and high
opinion of himfelf, though he fometimes
affects modefty, he introduced himfelf to
Lord S. and me; and under one pretence
or other, contrived to ftay a fortnight at
Glamis; during which time, he did every
thing to ingratiate himfelf, and fucceeded
fo well, that he could not help perceiv-
ing the progrefs he had made: and
indeed, when he preffed me to it, I partly confeffed it. Luckily his fifter was
ftaying with me; fo we never were alone,
but us three walking a whole morning,
to the amount of feveral miles meafured,
in the great hall at Glamis, every turn
he marked with a pencil. I had my hand
on a piece of paper he pinned up at the
end of the hall, which paper and pencil,
unluckily

unlucky a very remarkable one, he told me he would preferve as his life; but I hope he has loft it. I am not fure, but I have reafon to think, he got fome of my hair from his fifter. He was ordered to London to join his regiment.

Mr. Graham, of Fuitry, did not know of my liking for his brother; but as his affiftance was abfolutely neceffary in getting the money conveyed to London, which I was bent on fending him as from an unknown; Mifs G. told him that, out of friendfhip for her, and thinking her brother James a very promifing young man, I meant to fend him fome money to fpend in London: accordingly, he affifted her in forwarding it to him. Mifs Graham contrived a way for us to correfpond, which, though the letters were intercepted,

tercepted, nothing could be difcovered, as
we fixed initials quite different from the
real names ; by which we fignified our-
felves, and the people we had ofteneft
occafion to mention : and when I meant
to tell her any thing, or fhe to me, always
faid C. L. bid me tell A. B. fo and fo. I
burnt all her letters as I received them,
which I am now forry I did, and I de-
manded the fame of her; but fhe begged of me earneftly to let her keep, for
her perufal and entertainment, fometimes
thofe parts of my letters which did not concern her brother:—that, I would not refufe
her, promifing me fhe would burn or de-
face every word concerning him, and
fhewing me a letter for an example of
what fhe faid.

I faw

I faw Mr. James. Graham in London after he left Scotland, juft before he failed for Minorca; but found him much altered towards me, and therefore my pride made me treat him with the indifference I ought, though it almoft broke my heart. This is all, and far too much, of this foolifh affair.

I had almoft forgotten to mention, that Mifs Graham told me, the fecond of her three brothers (David) was a great admirer of mine, and perpetually talking of me; and that when he did, his eyes ufed to dart fire, and fparkle like diamonds (thefe were her very words) but I had only her word for thinking he had any partiality for me. He was ftill handfomer than either of his brothers (my favourite was the leaft fo) but before I was fcarce

acquainted

acquainted with David, I was fo taken up
with James, that I paid no attention to
him. James has or had a picture of me,
which he drew himfelf from memory;
and I am told by the few who faw it,
that it refembles me more than any picture which was ever taken of me. I
ought to tell you, why I faid Mrs. G. was
not good and virtuous: I am convinced,
fhe did Mifs Douglas's (Emelia) memory
a great injuſtice, and in a moſt treacherous
manner; for I am fure it fprang from
her. She then quarralled with Mrs.
Mylne, an amiable woman, and univer-
fally refpected, becaufe her eldeſt brother
married her fecond daughter; an agree-
able good girl, but with no fortune: and
before this, fhe ufed to profefs juſt the
fame friendſhip and difintereſted friendfhip fhe afterwards did for me; which
had

had fhe been a man, was feemingly fo
violent, I fhould have called it love. She
was very deceitful and cunning, and, I
believe, had an intrigue with Mr. Demp-
fter: fhe would with Mr. Nairn, had he
chofen.

I afked Mr. and Mrs. Stephens, at the
fame time, for fome of their hair (I think
they were together, but of that cannot be
pofitive) when I afked them. I afked alfo
Mr. Matra for a lock of his. Mr. Stephens had a ring compofed, half of Mrs.
Stephens's hair and half of mine; it is
quite plain, not fet round with any thing.
I cannot be certain whether I gave it him,
or whether he got it himfelf—I think I
gave it him myfelf; it was immediately
after his marriage: but what puzzles my
pofitive recollection is, that I know about

L   that

that time, Mrs. Stephens aſked me for
ſome of my hair, which I gave her. She
told me, ſoon after, that ſhe intended giving George Walker ſome preſent, for the
trouble he had about Mr. ——— and her
letters; and that ſhe intended giving him
a breaſt-locket, with her own hair ſet in
one part of it, and a bit of mine with it,
and that ſhe had ſome of it by her;
which, as ſhe could not afford to make
him a great preſent of intrinſic value,
ſhe thought nothing could be more accep-
table to ſo faithful a ſervant. I told her,
as I then thought, that he certainly was
ſo, and had been of great uſe to Mr. G.
and me; but, that I thought it an odd
preſent, theſe were my very words; and
as I ſaid no more, ſhe beſpoke it, and
when it was finiſhed, the addition of the
piece of hair, which was very ſmall and

covered

covered with glafs, prevented its faften-
ing: fo it was returned, and Mrs. Stephens got one ready made at a pawnbroker's fhop, one day when fhe and me walked into the city, out of curiofity to fee
thofe kind of fhops, and called at a great
number: at one of them, I bought a watch
which I gave George.—I gave George,
about this time, fome very old horfe furniture; which, though quite fpoilt, be-
fides being infinitely too antiquated for ufe,
contained fo much filver, that if I do not
miftake, it fold for upwards of 20l.: Mrs.
Parifh had difpleafed me fo much, and, apt
as I am to be impofed on, had fhewn fuch
proofs of a dirty interestednefs, that I determined to part with her; but, as fhe had
lived with, and partly educated me fo
many years, was refolved it fhould be on
good terms; therefore, I'refolved to raife

2000l.

2000l. by any means, the firſt money I expended. This, I thought, would be ſufficient to make her eaſy in circumſtances, if ſhe was intereſted as I thought her, or, if it was poſſible I had been miſtaken in her character, convince me by her ſtill remaining with me, that I had done her injuſtice. This I concealed from my mother, till I put it in execution, being greatly diſpleaſed at her offer of lending me 500l. when ſhe knew, what diſtreſs I was in, and that ſuch a ſum would do nothing for me. I even denied to my mother, when I gave Mrs. Pariſh the 2000l. (which I did at Paul's Walden, borrowing it of Mr. Peele, when he came there after Lord S.'s death, ſome time before I returned to town) and my mother believed I did not entertain the moſt diſtant

tant

tant thought that she would leave me, except by marrying.

As Mrs. Parish's conduct to me has been, her sister's excepted, the most vile, ungrateful, and pernicious, that ever was heard of, I shall say nothing about it here, as, during the whole, I cannot tax myself with doing any thing wrong; and this paper is only meant as a confession of my crimes and faults. But, if you please, I will tell you every circumstance relating to her behaviour, and to the strange manner she behaved to Mr. G. when, at his earnest request, he thinking she might be of use to me, I consented to his talking to her, and attempting to persuade her to stay with me, as from himself.

Just

Juſt before ſhe left me, I went to Paul's
Walden, to tell my mother I was married,
that I might get the ſtart of Mrs. Pariſh,
who, I was ſure, would write to tell her
the very day after our parting was agreed
on; and who, I believe, had it not been
for intereſted motives, and the fear of dif-
pleaſing my mother, would have told her
long before, which I have many reaſons
to be certain ſhe did not. I did not intend to declare my marriage till April, juſt
before we left England, or to be married
actually till we were abroad, a ſhort time
before I laid in; and I propoſed to ſtay
three or four years to viſit France, Italy,
Hungary, and Bohemia, and perhaps
Spain and Portugal : I did not tell even
Mr. Gray, poſitively, my deſigns about
marriage.

But

But I had almoft forgotten, that the reafon why I mentioned the 200ol. and Mrs.
Parifh, was, that I might tell you, foon
after I came out of town after Lord S.'s
death, I was perpetually fending George
backwards and forwards to London, to
raife the 200ol. After I applied to Mr.
Mayne, (who faid, he could not lend me
that fum without his partner's concur-
rence), I then applied to Fernandez, and
a number of other Jews, who did not
know me, and I did not fign my name to
the letter; but they would not lend me
on any other terms than annuities, which
I would not think of, and they were
dreadfully unreafonable ones. If I could,
I would have raifed three thoufand pounds,
to have had one thoufand pounds in hand.
When George went backwards and for-

wards

wards to thefe Jews, I ufed always to write
to, and hear from Mr. G. who ftayed juft
about that time after me in town. When
I was at Paul's Walden, and he in Scotland, all his letters to me came under
cover to George, and he always directed
mine to him; and under fome pretence
or other, went to Welwyn, Stephenage,
Hitchin, or Hatfield, and put them in
himfelf.

When I came occafionally to Paul's
Walden, for a week or a few days, once
or twice a fortnight, after I was fettled in
town, I ufed to enclofe my letters often,
under cover to George, (whom, on that
account, I generally left in town) and with
it, directions fometimes to him, to fend
meffages, or deliver notes about plays,
operas, dinings, tea-drinking, &c. and

often

often inclofed directions to the houfe-keeper of affairs relating to the houfe, &c. and fometimes I enclofed to George under the frank to her, and bid her give it once or twice. I remember, that having enclofed a number of letters and notes, to be delivered out, I faid, Go and tell Mr. G. I have no time to write now, but fhall be in Grofvenor-fquare, and expect him at fuch an hour. When Mrs. Ste-phens eloped, and I came to Paul's Wal-den, I left George in town to receive the Planta family, and fend me a conftant account of their motions ; which he did : I wifh I had kept them, as you might have liked to fee them ; but being, as I thought, of no confequence after fhe re-turned and knew the accounts, I burnt them.

M

Mr. Mylne, whose sister married Mr.
G. only lent Lord S. 10,000l. the half of
what he is worth ; and though the phy-
sicians declared her life was in danger, if
she did not go to Italy for her health directly (where I believe she now is) he was
threatened to be stopped by Lord S.'s creditors, who would come upon him. In
this situation, he desired Mr. G. when he
saw him in Scotland, and who he knew
had long been an acquaintance of mine,
to write to me, and beg I would allow
him to use my name, and say, I would
see the money should be paid out of the
Scotch estates, and the first debt dis-
charged. Mr. G. told him, he could not
possibly take such a liberty with me ; es-
pecially as he had not written to me even
a letter of condolance, as civility requir-
ed, since Lord S.'s death. But Mr. Mylne

preffed

preffed him fo much, and conjured him, as he regarded his fifter's life; that, not to make it appear fufpicious by too pofitive refufing, he wrote me a formal letter, and, at the fame time a private one, (both of which I am pretty fure are returned, and I can fhew you) and I anfwered him in the fame way: to Mr. Mylne I wrote a civil letter, telling him Mr. G. had informed me of his wifhes; that I was forry it was not in my power to fee his money paid which was due to him, as I had refufed taking adminiftration; but that if it was abfolutely neceffary, my regard for Mrs. Mylne, who is indeed an amiable woman, would induce me to join with him in being fecurity to his creditors: however, he never, after writing me a letter of thanks, claimed any offer, and got abr very well without it.

I c

I confefs, I fhould not have thought it neceffary, or any part of my agreement, to tell you the reafon why I faw Mr. G. only every other night, had you not defired I would: it was fo agreed on between us, that by the intervention of one night, we might meet the next with more plea-fure, and have the lefs chance of being tired of each other. Not to mention, that as it was often four or five in the morn-ing before he went away, a night of fleep was abfolutely neceffary: as our converfa-tion was to be lafting, and I generally went to my room at eleven o'clock the night he came, which I thought would look odd, and fometimes put me to difficul-ties, if I was at the Opera in a great croud, had company fupped with me, or any other hindrance; and I always contrived that fhould not be the cafe the nights he

came :

came : I faw him fome part of every day, or when I did not by any accident, he never failed writing.

A black inky kind of medicine (which I have mentioned before) occafioned two of my mifcarriages : the third, after trying the black medicine without effect, was occafioned by a vomit of emetic ; eating much pepper, and drinking a wine-glafs of brandy. I am afhamed to fay, I tried all thefe things the fourth time, without the fmalleft effect.

I do affure you, that no man ever took the fmalleft liberty with me (Lord S. yourfelf, and Mr. G. excepted) except three or four times that Mr. Stephens kiffed me, under one pretence or other; and once or twice that Mr. G. S. as we were ftanding

by

by the fire fide, put his arm round my
waift. Once, alfo, as I was admiring
fome very fcarce and valuable plants at
Hammerfmith, Mr. Lee told me, if I
would allow him the honour to falute a
Countefs, he would give me the moft cu-
rious; which I did, and had the plant.
I recollect once, that Mrs. Stephens fitting
on one of her hufband's knees, I fat on
the other.

Mr. G. S. I know, was free in his way
of thinking and acting; but his brother
I thought a different man, from fome
things I had heard him fay; and which
Mrs. Matra told me. Two or three times
Mr. Stephens has come into my room,
when my maid was dreffing my hair, and
I took him into my bed-room, out of the
drawing-room, where Mr. G. M. was to
fpeak

fpeak about going off with Mrs. Stephens.

Many of the things thefe papers contain, I have had an opportunity of telling you fince I began to write them, which I did not intend to do, till you read them here: other things you have, in the courfe of the fame time, told me you was thoroughly acquainted with : however I would not alter, and I give you my thoughts exactly, as they firft prefented themfelves to me, as you will eafily perceive I wrote no rough copy.

My almoft ftarving myfelf to death at Glamis; my taking, in anger, almoft a whole bottle of that black medicine; my foolifh behaviour about the cloaths and favours I befpoke for Mr. Stephens's wedding;

ding; the dancings on that occafion ; my allowing Mr. Stephens to call me his own wife; my worfe than foolifhnefs in going to St. Paul's with Mrs. Stephens and Mr. Pennick; and my making an excufe (with the laft defert of chriftening fome kittens) to have company to dine with me that day: all this knowing you are thoroughly informed of, I do not give more minutely than thus, on that account; nor fhould I have named them at all, had it not been for the oath's fake, which I could not fatisfy my confcience in taking, if I omitted, at leaft mentioning, any one of even the moft trifling imprudencies I committed.

I have told you of Mr. C. W. having my hair and I his ; and you know what a filly, though fhort refufal, I wrote to Mr. Mac Callafter, the autumn (I think it

was)

was) before my marriage—To his laſt, I
gave him no anſwer.

I have now fully performed my promiſe,
and I rely on your's to excuſe all my faults,
except want of veracity, which I am certain you cannot find here, and never ſhall
again, even in the moſt trifling matter:
as I will always rather prefer incurring
your more than uſual ſhare of diſlike to
me, than ſay what is not true.

You ſaw a bit of theſe papers laſt night,
when you came into my dreſſing-room,
though I begged you would not look, and
was angry at my minuteneſs, and telling
you ſuch trifles: if I had done otherwiſe,
(beſides my oath) might you not with juſ-
tice, and would you not have ſaid, I ordered you to be exact, minute, and ſcru-

N   pulous;

pulous; fo as to declare every thought that you had; were not thefe your own words? And how did you know what I fhould efteem trifling? Therefore, my deareft, you fhould excufe this minutenefs, and whatever manner I may mention the facts in, fo they be but facts!

God blefs you, and forgive me all my fins and faults.

FEBRUARY 3d, 1778. Tuefday morning.

I have had, you know, the paper you gave me in my pocket-book thefe three or four days; but, according to your orders, never looked at it till now. In confequence of what you here fay, I find myfelf obliged to fay fomething more about my fits, to which I did not intend, other-

wife,

wife, to have added any thing. If I were
to fay, as you feem to require of me, that I
ever could prevent or fhorten them, and
did not, except the one time I have mentioned, I fhould take my oath of a lie.

When I was a girl, I had two or three
times obftructions, and then I took, as it
were, common hyfteric fits; but I never
had them fo violent, or any thing like
convulfions, till four months that I had
an obftruction after my fecond or third
child, I forget which. And though my
mind was perfectly eafy at that time, I
being in Scotland, and had always company that I liked, yet I fuffered incredi-
bly from thefe fits, both in health and
looks; being exceedingly reduced and
weakened. I really believe it was owing
to Dr. Fergufon's prefcriptions, and to the

N 2   eafy

eafy ftate of my mind and good fpirits,
that I recovered ; but I have been fubject
to them ever fince. Dr. Hunter knows,
about three years ago or four, how much
I fuffered in my looks from them ; when
he was fent for to me the day after I had
been in one very bad, (no affectation) had
you feen me after, you would have been
convinced, would have affected a perfon
both at the fame time and afterwards, as
it has often done me. Sometimes when
I have had warning, which is not often,
I have ftopped the fit, by plunging my
hands into cold water, and fometimes by
drinking hot water or camomile tea. The
time you went to Newcaftle ; after that,
when on your return you found me fo ill,
I felt myfelf going to be ill ; and having
warning enough to drink a bafon of warm
water, and plunging my hands in cold
water,

water, I prevented the fit coming on; but
I never durſt mention it till now, left you
ſhould ſay it was an affeƈtation or air that
I gave myſelf.

What you ſay Dr. Scott told you about
my fits being pretended, and not a natural
complaint, was as falſe, as I dare ſay his
ſaying my miſcarrying was, when I had
that flooding, the firſt time of my being
regular after my lying-in; for you always took (at leaſt I never perceived you
did in the leaſt otherwiſe) a moſt certain
precaution. I remember Dr. Scott aſked
me once, if not twice, whether I did not
think I might have miſcarried; I ſaid, I
could not tell, but thought only a flooding; for you may be ſure, I would not
hint, or even have him ſuſpeƈt, that there
was any reaſon why I could not have miſcarried.

carried. To the beft of my recollection, he queftioned me on this fubject, one day when you brought him into the bed-room, and flipped yourfelf into the dreffing-room for a minute, and not the moment I conclude you mean; that is, when he faying you fent him, which you was angry at that time; upon the matureft recollection, I can venture to fay, he did not afk me that queftion, or any other about my health, except in general terms, how I did; fomething about my dinner, and mentioned the weather, or fome fuch fubject. You wanted an explanation, or fhould not have written this.

N B. Though I do not recollect, I declare upon oath, Mr. Stephens kiffing me oftener than I have mentioned; my fitting on his knee oftener; or Mr. G. S.

putting

putting his arms oftener round my waiſt, and that was by accident; yet I have ſuch a dread of the poſſibility of perjuring myſelf, that I will not take my oath without a proviſo, I really believe a needleſs one, that they may have repeated theſe liberties oftener, but never any others; except Mr. Stephens ſhaking me by the hand.

May I never feel happineſs in this world, or the world to come; and may my children meet every hour of their lives unparalleled miſery, if I have, either directly or indirectly, told one or more falſehoods in theſe narratives; or if I have kept any thing a ſecret, that even Mr. Bowes could eſteem a fault.

This

This I give under my hand, and shall never plead forgetfulness, or any thing else, for the truth of one tittle of it. And I do further swear the truth of it upon the Holy Bible: and as a declaration of my sincerity, shall take the Holy Sacrament upon it the next time I go to church, when there is one.

GIBSIDE, Feb. 3, 1778.

Examined with the Exhibit, contained in the Process transmitted from the Arches Court of Canterbury, this Fourth Day of October, 1788. By me, T. DODD, Clerk to Mr. Morley, Proctor, Doctor's Commons.

FINIS.